# WHITE FEATHER
## A Journey to Peace

BOOKS BY SUZANNE STUTMAN

*My Other Loneliness: Letters of Thomas Wolfe and Aline Bernstein*. Edited, and with an Introduction by Suzanne Stutman. Chapel Hill: University of North Carolina Press, 1983.

*Holding on for Heaven: Postcards and Cables of Thomas Wolfe and Aline Bernstein*. Edited, and with an Introduction by Suzanne Stutman. Special Publication of the Thomas Wolfe Society, 1985.

*The Good Child's River* by Thomas Wolfe. Edited, and with an Introduction by Suzanne Stutman. Chapel Hill: University of North Carolina Press, 1991.

*The Party at Jack's* by Thomas Wolfe. Edited and with an Introduction by Suzanne Stutman and John L. Idol, Jr. Chapel Hill: University of North Carolina Press, 1995.

*Broken Feather: A Journey to Healing*. By Suzanne Stutman. Philadelphia: Manor House Publications, Inc., 1996.

*A Passage to England: A Selection*. By Thomas Wolfe. Edited and with an Introduction by Suzanne Stutman and John L. Idol, Jr. Special Publication of the Thomas Wolfe Society, 1998.

# WHITE FEATHER
## A Journey to Peace

**By**

**Suzanne Stutman**

Manor House Publications, Inc.

Philadelphia, PA

# WHITE FEATHER
## A Journey to Peace


**Library of Congress Cataloging-in-Publication Data**

Stutman, Suzanne
White feather: a journey to peace / by Suzanne Stutman. –1st ed.
p. cm.
ISBN 0-9648261-4-3 -ISBN 0-9648261-5-1 (pbk.)
1.Peace–Poetry. 2. Peace movements–Poetry. I. Title.

PS3569.T884W47 2004
811′.54–dc22

2003070613

First Edition 2004
Manufactured in the United States of America

*To all of the children,*
*young and old,*
*who quest for peace.*

# CONTENTS

PART II: I AM UNIQUE IN ALL CREATION



PART III: I, A WOMAN

# PROLOGUE

## Take Back the Night

She cries out to me,
the child within myself.
She clutches at me,
tugging at my thoughts,
and asking to be remembered,
Her small fingers reach through time,
and her sad, dark eyes
burn the symbol of her pain
onto my soul.

For the child I was, for all of my fellow survivors, and most of all, for the children, I remember:

After my uncle hurt me, he would leave a quarter on the bureau. And after he left I would hide it. And the next day I would spend it. If I think back really hard, I can remember the feel of those quarters clutched so tightly in my hand. I didn't know then that he was making me a part of a conspiracy, a secret, that I would pay dearly for in pain and shame for so many years of my life. I remember. Before I would fall asleep,

I would stare at the ghost of the door. It was formed by the light coming through from the hallway. If I watched it and tried not to blink or not close my eyes, then it wouldn't move—or so I hoped. Every night in that room I lay, eyes wide open, watching, praying that the ghost would not move. It wasn't until so many years later that I came to understand that I was waiting for the door to open, frozen in fear and helplessness, and praying that it would not and that I would be safe for one more night.

I tried to tell, but no one was listening. And I cried a lot, but my tears seemed silent, not to make a difference. So I stopped trying to tell—and I really didn't have the words anyway to say what was happening to me. I felt invisible. And I fell silent, thinking that what was happening was the way of things, and that I was being punished for being bad, and that I was indeed the ugliest, the stupidest, the baddest person in the whole world.

I believed that for some reason what was happening was supposed to happen. That I was supposed to hurt like this. So I got up and changed the sheets during the night, or put a towel on my bed to cover the wet spots. And I complained a lot of stomachaches and didn't want to go to school. And I was always afraid, because I never knew when it was going to happen. And I felt so different from everybody else because I had this terrible secret I had to keep, and I was an ugly, bad and awful person. But I would try to be better. I would try to make people love me. But I was so alone. And I didn't know how.

When I was a little girl I had no voice. I was invisible. Nobody listened. All that is changed now. And I raise my voice on behalf of the children, so that they don't have to suffer anymore.

Shadow man,

dripping darkness.

Coming softly,

moving darkness.

Looming dark,

moving shadow.

You steal

into

my

fear

until

my silent

screams

illuminate

you.

And I,

transfixed,

electrified,

am forced

to die.

Again.

I didn't really know what it was that pained me, but I felt that it was a natural and necessary part of my inner self. I also felt that for some reason I had to hide it, that it was for some reason dangerous to show, even to the people who loved me the most, how much I was afraid, how little I really liked myself, and most of all, my anger.

I cannot begin to explain to you the fear. I would wake up with it. I would go to sleep with it. It would awaken me in the night. And that was the worst time. Something was going to happen—and I didn't know what it was. I kept closet doors closed, but not before I looked into closets before I went to sleep. I looked under the bed. I kept the light on in the bathroom, because I understood that darkness was my enemy. What I understood deeply was that no one was really to be trusted. That anything could change at any moment. That I had to fight very hard to be loved because I wasn't really worthy of it, so I had to be good, very good, always good. And I could never really let my guard down. From the earliest time came the lesson. No one must ever know.

I became in my home and in my teaching, and in fact in most every situation, a defender. Knowing what it was like to be invisible, I found myself fighting for the rights of those who were treated in any way lesser than. And because I had experienced so little true kindness in my early life, I understood always the magnificence of the simplest act of mercy. Kindness, gentleness—seemed to me the greatest balance in life. And I must say, they still do. To give to those who may not have visibility, who may not have love, moments, space, the strength of telling—these are the lessons I learned from the silent world around me. These are the lessons I learned from my deepest self. So in trying to heal myself, I came to understand instinctively the importance of the healing balance of caring. I became a mother, then I became a teacher. From both I learned to stop the world. To try to make it, in my own private sphere, a clean, well-lighted place. To do for others what was rarely done for me.

I began to write my story in poems and sketches and entitled my book *Broken Feather: A Journey to Healing*. I would write the pieces, or they would write me, and each time I finished I would understand more about myself; I would hold in my hands another small piece of the past. For so long I had been teaching the voices of others: Now I was writing my testimony, bringing my voice out of the darkness. I came to understand that there was no going back. I would have to break the silence. Big Time.

I have found in each encounter with others who have been victimized, men and women, the boys and girls in them still locked in pain, that what happens to those of us who are abused as children is often much the same. I have heard tales of horror. Tales of fear. Tales of rejection. Over the past year and a half I have heard so many stories—indeed, everywhere I go others share their stories—often in secret. And I think always—why is it we who are not believed? Why must these horrors of abuse which can diminish a soul for a lifetime not be shared? Why cannot this secret be brought to light? What is wrong with this society when the victim is to blame and the abuser is free to hurt again?

Which brings me to the next step in my journey. In this short time I have found a new advocacy: I advocate for survivors, to let them know that they are loved, that they are not alone. That the healing journey is indeed possible. That it is o.k. to tell. And the big lesson. The one it takes so long to really believe. That it is not their fault, what happened. It is not our fault.

I have done fundraisers for various child abuse prevention agencies, nationally and internationally, and a major portion of the proceeds of my book goes to benefit these agencies. I am on the Board of Friends of the Children, a group of volunteers which works to help fund The Center for Children's Support in Stratford, N.J. Some of my new poems have been on display at UNICEF House, serving as my interpretation of the exquisite artworks of abused children from the Center for Children's Support. I have been working since August in an afterschool program for disadvantaged children, and I go into area high schools to talk to teen mothers, some who have histories of abuse, to let them know that they are not alone. I have come to understand that I must use my power to try to build power in others.

I have learned through my own life to take back the night. And I ask you, particularly you students, you who are our best and our brightest, to empower yourselves to do the same. Do not believe that one person can't make a difference. If you make a difference in one life—you have stopped the world.

It is the aloneness of abuse which is part of what is so terrible. It isolates, it denegrates, it makes us feel that we are bad, and ugly and useless—and the list goes on. In fact, those of us who have been so wounded have our own kind of beauty: we understand pain and invisibility and vulnurability and silence. We have often the passion and the compassion to reach out to others, to try with every ounce of strength within us to take the pain away. This is our gift. For we are like the pheonix risen from the ashes. We must make the day bright for those not as strong as we have become. We must march, we must protest, we must legislate, we must raise our voices into the darkness so that no child be allowed to fall, no victims suffer in silence and shame. In so doing we take back the night.

— Suzanne Stutman

*This speech was first presented at Penn State University, University Park, in April 1998.*

# INTRODUCTION

## White Feather: A Journey to Peace
## The Healing Art of Poetry

I have always wanted to make the pain go away. From the time I was the littlest child and used to sneak with bottles of milk out of my back door, bowl in hand, to feed the strays who lived in my neighborhood, there has been an inspiration, I believe, to fill, if not the belly, then the soul. To make people feel good about themselves. To bring smiles, and a feeling of deep self-respect. To make the sun shine in somebody's heart. To be a healer. I believe with my whole heart and soul that love is the greatest healer of all. And that hope is as much a part of us as the air we breathe. And that we are all exquisite in our complexity, and each of us, unique and beautiful.

Because I am a survivor of trauma in my early life, I carry the wound within me. I understand deeply fear and sadness and guilt and shame and anger and silence. And most of all, loneliness. For to suffer trauma seems to feel as if it separates us away from others, makes us different—unlovable—unreachable—at times, even to ourselves.

But we are not different. Sometimes I think that we are just deeper, perhaps, than others who may have not been tested in the same way. And I think that the challenge is to connect the broken parts back together inside us. To shine a light into our deepest souls. To become infinitely curious about who we are and what we think and why we feel the ways we do. To become students of ourselves. To marvel at our complexity. To wonder at our imagination. To be awed by our courage. To cry tears of joy that we have survived to breathe the air, smell the flowers, feel the wind, watch the snow: to just exist.

Let us carry hope in our pocket, and when we are tired or hurting, let us take it out and stare into its center, and feel peace inside.

These poems have been written, donated and displayed at conferences and on behalf of national and international organizations. Among them: Friends of the Children, The Center for Children's Support, The Philadelphia Children's Alliance, Heartbeat- South Africa, The International Health Awareness Network, The International Medical Women's Association, The International Council of Women, The National Council of Women of the United States and South Africa Age-In-Action. They have been presented and displayed at the United Nations in New York, as well as in Australia,

Switzerland, Thailand, South Korea, South Africa, and at various locations in the United States.

May these poems reflect and celebrate mankind's tentative yet inexorable journey toward peace.

– Suzanne Stutman
October 2004

# PART I

# THE VOICE OF A CHILD

# People I Know

People

I

know

and

love

are

not

supposed

to

hurt

me.

I

am

too

help

less

to

know

this

is

wrong.

So

I

lie

down,

and

I

feel

pain

and

shame.

I

die.

I

am

so

afraid.

Only

when

I

tell

can

I

grow

Big

again,

and

my

Smile

can

gobble

up

the

World.

## You Made Me Ashamed

You

made

me

ashamed

of

my

body.

So

I

must

hide

my

Self.

I

can

only

look

down,

now,

fearfully,

or

back,

over

my

shoulder.

I

am

so

ugly.

I

can

trust

no

one.

# The Voice of a Child

I

am

eternal

springtime.

When

you

hurt

me

and

I

bleed,

my

tears

flow

over

the

Earth.

My

sadness,

voiceless,

pleads

to

be

heard.

And

the

Sun

sinks

in

protest.

# I Opened My Self Up

I

opened

my

self

up,

and

I

gave

you

my

Heart.

You

took

my

smile

and

turned

it

upside

down,

dripping

Red

tears.

Now

I

know

only

sadness.

I

am

small

enough,

now,

to

hold

my

self,

eyes

closed

from

the

world,

and

cry

for

what

could

have

been.

# When I Am Whole

When

I

am

whole

inside,

Earth

dances,

the

Sun

shines

over

the

world.

Joy

bubbles

up

and

smiles

like

dolphins

swimming

in

a

sparkling

sky.

# Hope

When

I

am

happy,

all

the

Earth

sings

with

me.

Flowers

burst

with

joy,

birds

circle

the

Sky,

and

life

has

meaning

for

Everyone.

For

I

deserve

no

less

than

this:

Peace

and

Happiness.

## If I Could Speak

If

I

could

speak,

I

would

say,

"Please

Don't

Hurt

Me!"

I

would

write

upon

my

body,

"Do

Not

Touch."

I

would

wish

that

you

would

see

my

blackened

eyes,

my

bruised

face

and

arms

and

legs.

My

fear

and

anger,

like

a

plugged

chimney

on

the

top

of

my

head,

waits

to

Burst

from

me.

Why

won't

you

see

my

pain?

# The World is Angry

The

world

is

angry.

It

splits

my

heart

into

blood

and

darkness.

Violence

and

fear

coil

like

tentacles

onto

the

square

Earth.

I

am

upside

down,

hanging,

in

a

place

mis

shapen,

in

a

world

I

can

not

understand

# I Was at the Bottom of the World

I

was

at

the

bottom

of

the

world.

When

He

hurt

me,

tears

came

from

his

fingers.

The

clouds

cried

With

me.

Now

I

am

on

the

top

of

the

sky.

The

Sun

shines

for

me,

and

I

fly

with

the

birds.

I

can

grow

Up

now.

# Behind the Closed Door

Behind

the

closed

door,

he

hurt

me,

and

he

said

to

me,

"Don't

tell

your

mom."

My

house

fell

on

itself.

Everything

was

dark

and

upside

down.

It

was

not

Safe

anymore.

# Round and Black and Ugly

Round

and

black

and

ugly

is

the

silence

of

not

telling.

When

I

tell

and

people

listen,

I

can

come

out

of

my

hiding

place.

I

can

begin

to

Smile

and

bring

my

crying

self

back

from

the

darkness.

I

can

catch

Stars

and

put

them

in

my

pocket.

## Small in the Silence

Small

in

the

silence

I

have

no

voice.

But

when

I

tell

and

people

believe

me,

I

can

be

anything

I

want.

I

can

be

my

own

best

friend.

# PART II

# I AM UNIQUE IN ALL CREATION

## I Am Unique in All Creation

I

own

what

I

think

and

what

I

write

upon

a

page.

No one

can

think

exactly

like

I

do.

I am

Unique

in

all

Creation.

## My song

I am a child.

I know only
the sky and
the earth and
the sun.

My world is
the people who
love me,
Or who do not.

When I cry,
the world
does not listen.

It thinks
that

my cries

are not important,

that my tears

are in

a

Different

language.

I know only

that

I am hungry.

I am frightened.

I am cold.

I am weary

beyond my years.

I may die,

never knowing

the

Joy

of life.

When you sanction

my country,

you sanction

me.

You tell me

that

I don't exist.

That

I am worth

nothing.

That my song,

sailing

like a kite

over blue waters,

will never be

heard.

## Me, I, Myself

If I hold

my own hand,

I will have

a hand

to hold

onto.

If I love

my own

self,

I will have

a self

to love.

## Valentines

Poems

are

like

valentines

we

give

to

ourselves.

Expressions

of

love,

and

the

creative

spirit.

Poems

make

my

heart

sing.

They

connect

me

with

the

music

inside

myself.

They

help

me

to

bring

out

the

pictures

Inside

me.

They

make

my

heart

smile.

## The Dancing Leaf

We walked along the creek

one day,

and spoke of life

and

time,

and then,

we started on our walk

again.

We paused before

a

Great

old tree,

and marveled

at its

size

and

age.

It dwarfed us both,
and you
and I
Reflected on
the soft blue
sky
and on
the
gift
of
Life
gone by—
and that
we
formed
a

trinity—

a boy,

a

nonny

and

a

tree.

Then something

special

caught our

eye.

And neither of

Us—

you or I—

could quite

believe

what

we

Could

see:

A leaf

was

dancing!

Close we went,

and

closer yet,

until we touched it,

pulled it,

Tried

to

understand

how

this one leaf

remained,

sus

Pen

ded,

in

the

sky.

We searched for

strings, or webs

or sticks,

we entertained

the thought of

tricks:

And then we just

watched,

dazzled,

as

it

moved

about

by

its

own wits.

A living

Leaf

Performed

a

Dance:

and did

we

Happen

just

by

Chance

to

see

this

Magic?

Or did

we

share

a

moment's

time—

as

Angels

joined

us—

and

we

three —

were

Dancing,

While

The

World

passed

by,

just

waltzing

in

Eternity.

La.

# I Saw a Lumpy Bumpy Dumpy Grumpy Tree

I

saw

a

lumpy

bumpy

dumpy

grumpy

tree.

And he

said

to me:

"Go away.

I have

been

struck

by lightening,

stung

by bees,

invaded

by

squirrles

and

assorted

birds,

and

stared

at

by

humans.

I want

to

em

bark

on

a

journey

alone."

And with

that,

he raised

his

roots

up

out

of

the ground,

and

walked away.

# A Big Black Fuzzy Bumble Bee

A

big

black

fuzzy

bumble

bee,

mis

taking

me

for

a

flower,

flew

into

my

ear

and,

thinking

I

was

his

honey,

tickled

me.

When

he

realized

his

mis

fortune,

he

made

a

break

for

it,

buzzing

in

dig

nant

ly

up,

into

the

sky.

And

I,

stung

by

rejection,

cried

tears

which

fell

onto

the

flowers,

and

watered

their

morning.

## Well, Miss Octa Puss

Well,

Miss

Octa

Puss,

Sitting there

so

smug,

Stuck

between

two

rocks,

Floating

In the

water's breeze:

Don't

you

know

how

lucky

you are

To be able

to

Fit

into

anything?

# PART III

# I, A WOMAN

## I, a Woman

Sometimes I wonder

why

I,

a

Woman,

must

suffer

such

pain.

I,

who

was

created

to

bear

children,

to

love

Earth

and

its

creatures,

to

nurture

and

preserve.

Why

must

my

eyes

be

bruised

and

beaten?

Why

must

my

body

be

torn

by

rape,

my

babies

be

taken

from

my

womb

without

my

sanction?

Why

must

they

tear

from

me

my

soul,

circumcision

into

pain

and

grief

and

sometimes,

Death.

I

who

am

only

a

woman:

Flower

of

the

Earth.

## Life, Eternal

I

who

am

the

womb

of

Earth,

I

who

hold

the

wings

and

heart

of

Peace,

I

am

dying.

Night

surrounds

me.

Death

overcomes

me.

I

am

Blinded;

my

tears,

like

tattered

feathers,

bleed

into

the

sea,

meteors

of

grief,

doomed

fish,

entering

the

darkness.

I

am

the

Waves

of

the

great

Oceans,

the

Soul

of

the

Rivers.

Please

do

not

kill

me.

You

kill

yourselves.

## Old Woman

Once,

there

was

Hope.

Earth

sang

and

the

wind,

smiling,

danced

all

night.

Now

there

is

only

sadness.

Earth

bleeds,

trees

pierce

the

sky,

and

I

hear

only

screams

of

the

dead

and

dying.

My

head

holds

rivers

of

Tears.

Dead

babies

kiss

dead

mothers.

Unborn.

Unborning.

Raped.

Entombed.

Good

men,

lost,

hold

only

to

my

mind's

grey

litanies:

Tattered

umbrellas

in

a

scorched

desert.

How

do

I

live

with

this.

When

do

I

die.

# War

Baby

boy,

you

crawled

into

the

Sun,

and

it

exploded,

like

a

ball

of

pain.

Little

girl,

I

can

still

hear

you

laugh

as

you

run

into

the

sky.

Then

why

did

the

Stars

burst?

Did

you

fall

into

a

spiraling

universe,

only

to

be

spit

forth,

into

a

new

World:

Whirling

through

space.

Erased

by

dull

plants

rotting

in

the

earth,

blossoming

death?

# Mother

Like

a

flower,

your

body

grows:

Breasts

petal—

soft

and

full

of

the

fluid

of

life,

rising

from

the

very

womb

of

earth

to

nourish

you.

So

that:

You

can

feed

your

Child.

Holy,

this

nurturing.

Holy

are

you,

Mother,

who

become

your

own

prayer,

a

song

of

love

for

all
the
children.

From
your
deep
red
heart,
you
fill
the
cup
of
the
world,
with
Peace.

## Baby

My

baby

is

a

blossom,

blooming

from

my

body

new

Life.

Mother

Earth

has

kissed

us,

and

given

us

her

Blessing.

## Brave

I

must

be

brave

now,

for

this

new

Life.

Like

the

lioness

I

must

protect:

my

self,

my

family,

my

Eternity.

## The Future

I

see

the

Future

in

your

face,

little

one:

happy

daughter,

strong

son.

I

will

raise

you

like

a

tree

in

the

forest:

so

that

you

can

greet

the

leaves

in

passing,

and

dream

the

Sky.

## When the Earth Breaks

My

soul

groans

like

the

Earth

breaking,

child,

when

you

are

ill.

I

must

become

Ancient

in

my

wisdom,

Fierce

in

my

Strength,

to

save

You.

# The Imposter

Woman,

you

look

so

lovely

tonight,

sleek

in

black

satin,

shoulders

punctuating

the

light

like

sharp

round

exclamations.

Your

hair

falls

over

your

eyes

and

into

your

face

like

a

baby

rocking

in

a

cradle.

Why

is

it,

then,

that

I

have

come

upon

you,

crying,

catching

by

surprise

the

little

girl

Lost

who

peeks

through

your

shattered

face:

dressed

up

in

mommy's

tears.

## Woman

Bright

like

a

star

is

your

gentle

face.

It

shines

hope.

It

sparkles

joy.

Your

eyes

Embrace

eternity.

Pouring

goodness

into

the

world's

cup.

Dipped

in

shining

Grace.

# PART IV

# ALL OF OUR HEARTS ARE ONE

# Wildflowers

Wildflowers

bloom

with in

my

mind.

Choirs

of

angels,

summoning

my

heart

and

eyes

to

silent

adulation.

Spring

has

awakened.

# In the Territory of My Soul

The

territory

of

my

soul

knows

no

boundaries.

Its

landscape

is

the

moon—

or

earth—

on

its

Best

day.

Its

music

is

the

singing

of

my

heart.

In

the

territory

of

my

soul,

I

find

Peace.

# I Count the Circles

I

count

the

circles

of

my

soul.

I

dance

the

drumbeat

of

my

heart.

I

string
the
hours
on
my
wrist.

And
watch
them
sparkle.

In
time's
procession,
I
carry
my
bouquet,

tossing

my

dreams

to

breathless

outstretched

hearts.

Singing

to

the

stars,

I

poise

in

flight:

Stopping

to

catch

tomorrow

with

my

wings.

## Nobody Told Me

Nobody

told

me

I

would

grow

old.

Nobody

told

me

I

would

Count

time

by

Green

trees

and

Blue

skies

and

Child's

eyes:

Nobody

told

me

I

would

grow

wise.

## Peace

If

I

could

weave

peace

into

the

fabric

of

the

world,

I

would

stitch

flowers

onto

its

hem,

and

shake

it

over

earth,

and

say,

"There, now,

Rest."

## The Dance

The

muffled

ancient

tribal

drums

beat

slowly

through

the

totemed

heart.

Their

sound

stirs

silent

memories

spun

softly

through

the

air tight

tombs.

Until

all

time

is

in

a

trance,

the

feathered

rhythm

of

the

dance,

and

self

is

lost

and

life

becomes

the

echoed

rhythm

of

the

drums.

# Hope

We stand here

on this shattered land

an army of

children.

And we march

to the tune

of

the earth's turning.

It sings

of

circles

in the sky.

Its truth

is

burning

in the round

sun

which

gives us life.

May we look

at the faces

of the moon

and

sing its praises.

May we form

a ring

and

dance

and

sing

to the music

of the turning

of the earth.

And when we must,

may we

look in to

the splendor

of

each other's face,

and wipe away

our tears.

## A Prayer for the Children

Dear God who makes all things grow,

Who gives us life.

Who allows us to meet with wonder

The birds in the sky,

The fish in the sea,

The great trees in the meadows.

Oh wondrous God,

I pray to you on behalf of the children.

May they grow strong and tall,

Like trees in the forest.

May their laughter fill the world

Like bells in the morning.

May they learn through words,

And books, to cultivate themselves

And their dreams, like farmers with

The most precious crops, sacred,

Each sacred, each a prayer in the morning.

May they learn:

The depths of their souls.

The reach of their minds.

May they dream dreams, and Make them

Come true.

## All of Our Hearts are One

Please don't tell me

I can't love you

Because your eyes

are a different color

than mine.

Because your skin

is a different color

than mine.

Because your God

Shines

in your soul

with a Light

that Seems different

than mine.

I reserve the Right to love you,

like I love the Sun.

You are life's Bloom:

You are my family:

my sister, my brother, my child.

In your heart lie the pieces of my soul.

# EPILOGUE

# ALL THE POWER RESTS WITH YOU

## All the Power Rests with You

You belong to yourself.

Celebrate the things that belong to you.

Nobody can take away from you what

belongs to you.

Clap your hands!

Stamp your feet!

Stretch your arms out as far as they can go,

And Dance.

Now dance in a circle.

Hug yourself.

Touch your nose.

Touch your toes.

Touch your ears.

Wiggle your eyebrows.

Make funny faces.

Make funny voices.

And Smile—the biggest smile you can!

Write a poem about your smile.

Write a poem about your toes.

Write a poem about your nose.

Think about all who love you.

The sky loves you.

The trees love you.

The rocks love you. Even the bugs that scamper to get away from the stamp of your feet, love you.

I love you.

God loves you.

Write some poems about the things who love you.

Write a poem about the sky.

Write a poem about a flower.

Write a poem about a tree.

Write a poem about the sea.

Now write a poem about yourself.

Sometimes things hurt you.

People can hurt you.

Things that happen can make you feel sad inside.

Write a poem about what hurts you.

Write a poem about what makes you sad.

And then REMEMBER to STAMP your feet,

And touch your ears

And touch your toes

And hug yourself with a very big smile.

Because!!!!!

Only you belong to you.

What's missing? Sometimes tears are

missing.

When we cry we water the sky.

Tears make things grow.

Sometimes, they make us grow inside,

because they tell us how we feel.

They are our way of talking to ourselves,

sometimes.

All of us feel sorry, when we are sad.

Sometimes, tears are necessary to let us

know that it's o.k. to feel sad sometimes.

Think of your favorite colors.

Write your colors.

Write a poem about each of your favorite

colors.

The world is made up of beautiful things.

You are one of the world's beautiful things.

Close your eyes. What colors do you see?

Open your eyes. What colors do you see?

Think of sounds.

Some sounds are good sounds.

Name the good sounds.

Name the bad sounds.

Write about the good sounds.

Write about the bad sounds.

What feels good?

Write about what feels good.

Write about what feels bad.

Remember. You belong to you.

You will always belong to you.

You will always have a friend.

Because you are your own friend.

You are your own, very own, very own,

best friend.

Anything you say to you is o.k.

Anything you feel inside you is o.k.

You can love you, and love you and love

you—as much as you want.

You belong to you, always and forever.

Think about babies.

Think about

New things

Small things

True things

Safe things.

Think about butterfly wings.

All the world belongs to you.

All the world belongs to you.

Believe this and you make it true.

All the power rests with you.

Touch your feelings.

How far do they go?

Can you touch them like you touch your

nose?

Do they stop at the end of your toes?

What makes you happy?

What makes you sad?

What makes you angry?

What makes you care?

What do you care about?

How rich you are!

How rich you are!

You own your eyes,

Your nose

Your ears

Your toes

Your hands

Your feet

Your smile

Your teeth!

You own all that you see and feel.

And if you feel it, then it's real.

You own the sky above your head.

You own the dreams you have at night.

You own the thoughts that sing inside.

You own the love that holds you tight.

You own tomorrow and today

And all the love that comes your way.

ALL THE POWER RESTS WITH YOU.